BURNING BABYLON

BY THE SAME AUTHOR

Soft Keys
Raising Sparks

BURNING BABYLON

Michael Symmons Roberts

*For Elaine,
with all best wishes,
MSR
[illegible] - Oct. 2001.*

CAPE POETRY

Published by Jonathan Cape 2001

2 4 6 8 10 9 7 5 3 1

Copyright © Michael Symmons Roberts 2001

Michael Symmons Roberts has asserted his right under the Copyright, Designs and Patents Act 1988 to be identified as the author of this work

This book is sold subject to the condition that it shall not, by way of trade or otherwise, be lent, resold, hired out, or otherwise circulated without the publisher's prior consent in any form of binding or cover other than that in which it is published and without a similar condition including this condition being imposed on the subsequent purchaser

First published in Great Britain in 2001 by
Jonathan Cape
Random House, 20 Vauxhall Bridge Road,
London SW1V 2SA

Random House Australia (Pty) Limited
20 Alfred Street, Milsons Point, Sydney,
New South Wales 2061, Australia

Random House New Zealand Limited
18 Poland Road, Glenfield,
Auckland 10, New Zealand

Random House South Africa (Pty) Limited
Endulini, 5A Jubilee Road, Parktown 2193, South Africa

The Random House Group Limited Reg. No. 954009
www.randomhouse.co.uk

A CIP catalogue record for this book
is available from the British Library

ISBN 0-224-06185-2

Papers used by Random House are natural, recyclable products made from wood grown in sustainable forests; the manufacturing processes conform to the environmental regulations of the country of origin

Typeset by Palimpsest Book Production Limited,
Polmont, Stirlingshire

Printed and bound in Great Britain by
Creative Print and Design (Wales), Ebbw Vale

For Joseph and Patrick

The buildings are set on fire, the bars of the gates broken.
Runner speeds to meet runner, messenger to meet messenger,
reporting to the King of Babylon that every quarter of his city is taken.

Jeremiah 51: 30–31

CONTENTS

I COLLATERAL DAMAGE

Touched	3
The Qualities of Fallout	4
Pika	5
Collateral Damage	6
Symptoms	7
The Opposites	8
The Qualities of Dust	9

II SORTIES

A Pilot's Coat	13
The Absence of War	15
Munitions	16
Sorties	17
Protect and Survive	18
The Baton	19
A Storm	20
Payload	21
Summer Advent	22

III FRIENDLY FIRE

Ground Zero	27
Dummy Runs	29
The Toe-Ring	30

The Star	31
Feast of the Innocents	32
Yule Ball	33
The Ram-Raid	34
Tented Village	35
A Ghost-Tree	36
The Sacrifice	37
Deposition	38
Friendly Fire	39
Melissa Jones	40
The List	41
Strange Meeting	42

IV HYPOCENTRE

Lament	45
The Disappeared	47
New Greenham Park	48
Woad	49
Restoration	50
Fauna	51
Second Strike	52
Warlords in Waiting	53
Common Toad	54
Endgame	55
Grave Goods	56
Deus Ex Machina I	57
The Fence	59
Remnant	60
Deus Ex Machina II	61
A Gift Horse	62
The Wanderer	63
Blackout	64

ACKNOWLEDGEMENTS

Acknowledgements are due to the following:
Grand Street, Guardian, Observer, Quadrant, The Reader

Various parts of this sequence were broadcast in various forms on BBC Radio 4 and the BBC World Service.

I
COLLATERAL DAMAGE

'Greenham and Crookham Commons sit on a gravel-capped ridge on the south side of the Kennet Valley, three miles from Newbury. The summit plateau was predominantly lowland heath, a habitat that has been vastly modified by the development of the airbase. What would have been a gently undulating landscape has been levelled. Material was imported onto the site to fill the many gullies that cut into the ridge. This import of material modified the soil pH and created new habitats.'

– Green Ways: Berkshire's Rights of Way Magazine,
Issue No. 4, Summer 1999

TOUCHED

When geiger's ungloved finger
brushes thorium, uranium,
its nervy click-tongue quickens
to a heart's-race, so it croons
the first note of a love song,
holds it, and forgets the rest.

THE QUALITIES OF FALLOUT

Would it be conspicuous as snowflakes,
only white-hot? Or subtle as

that valley rain, which drenches
without ever being other than the air?

Is it like cyanide – odourless
to half the world, burnt almonds to the rest?

Winter solstice. Deep advent.
Darkness is thicker than ever;

people are led through dry streets
by their dogs and their troubles,

and there is a new subtext to the sky,
something of cobweb, salt and star.

PIKA

Elusive, witnessed first on paper,
then in deserts, then one whole city.
Those on the outskirts called it
pikadon: flash-boom in Japanese.
Those who saw it closer shortened it
to *pika*: a flash without a voice.
Survivors said it entered them
through eyes, then mapped them
in an instant – silver and alive.
After that it went to one more city,
then back to sands and seas.

New Year's Day, Hiroshima, 1945:
outlandish snowfall for a warm
delta city. Seven great rivers,
seven dark threads in the blanket.
Bridges fill with marvellers.
Believers in ill omens keep
their mouths shut, for fear
of *tonarigumi*: keepers of morale.
Come summer everyone would know
that *pika* had prepared its way
with ice and painless beauty.

COLLATERAL DAMAGE

Snowlight. Cold made visible.
Cats dressage across the deep lawn
– impossibly luminous, *ex nihilo* –

and by the window, torn
between her living and her dead,
an old woman pulls the curtain.

Butterflies in glass blocks line the sill,
and relics of her sons in uniform,
those glazed too, and framed in steel.

SYMPTOMS

Once, when fevers here were scarlet,
they were healed in deep seclusion

in a sullen limewashed hospital
folded into alder, beech and gorse.

Now, in this our atom triangle
– Greenham, Burghfield, Aldermaston –

fevers are more subtle, no isolation
needed, just a silent vigilance.

Some of us cannot stop washing,
imagining the geiger count across our hands.

Some conjure bruises like armfuls of tattoos
that warn the base is in their blood.

THE OPPOSITES

Cold war skewed polarities,
so war meant peace;
both equally right and coterminous.
Cold was hot, light was dark.

On the knee-high
baseball field, the scoreboard,
in spite of blank
sockets and blind bulbs,

tells history now — *inning*, *ball*,
strike, *out* — and truth:
the team that played here
was both *home* and *visitors*.

It was an open secret:
civilians were soldiers,
friends could well be enemies,
life was sweet as salt.

THE QUALITIES OF DUST

Kicks up in clouds, coats shoes
with sudden history, settles on
cloth to be brushed off, but some
sinks in; turns fertile on a wet tongue,
gifted into taste and smell.
We were made of this,

and this is made of us; of skin
flakes and dry earth and famine.
Surely all that we remember
of each other will not end as this;
but if it does, may it, may we,
set light to other tongues.

II
SORTIES

'The three main blocks of vegetation on the airbase cover some 100 hectares and have a complex range of habitats within them. These include typical lowland heath, lichen heath, bare gravels, calcareous and neutral grassland. When the airbase was operational, these habitats were maintained by regular gang mowing.'

– Green Ways: Berkshire's Rights of Way Magazine,
Issue No. 4, Summer 1999

A PILOT'S COAT

Its cloth was so beautifully brushed and cut that he had to have it. The tunic was a parting gift to Lisa Jones from her pilot boyfriend, when his F1-11 squadron went home to Arizona. The missiles were coming, and missiles need no pilots. On the balmy June night when the squadron flew its nest, Lisa stepped out and put the jacket in the bin, then locked her bedroom door for two days. When Lisa's brother Jason saw it in among the garbage he fell in love. Not that he had liked Bill the pilot, or liked the USAF. He had no interest in planes either. It was just that the coat was immaculate, like a perfect mown lawn. He took it to his room and put it on. That night he slept in it.

★

That summer night when Jason Jones rescued a pilot's tunic from the bin, and took it to his room, he passed – between the back door and his bedroom door – his mother on the sofa in a Valium stupor; his father with notebooks fine-tuning a fruitless failsafe betting system for the horses; then the shade of his undead father on the stairs, the one who used to talk to his children before he was sacked from AWE Aldermaston for unspecified reasons. Then upstairs he passed his older sister Lisa's silent room; and his younger sister Melissa's shut door behind which – he knew – she lay awake and terrified.

★

When Jason took Bence and Leo back to his house after school, he offered them no food or drink, just led them straight up to his room and told them to sit on his bed. He lifted a box from the top of his wardrobe. Inside was a layer of tissue paper and a layer of bubble-wrap, and between them, some thick olive-green cloth. He lifted it out, and held it up, letting its own weight unfold it. An F1-11 pilot's jacket. Jason put it on, combed his hair in the mirror, then paraded up and down the room, half goose-stepping which made the others laugh.

He showed them the buttons, the braid, the lining. He went on about the jacket so much that Bence left. Leo stayed longer, and talked about the planes he had seen at the old Greenham Air Shows, but Jason was not interested in planes. He knew none of their names. He was not listening.

THE ABSENCE OF WAR

Early hours.
Sheet lightning
guts the common.
Its blade bounces
off the runway.
It lacks the pinpoint
jag of bolts or forks.

This charge is
thunderless, edgeless.

In similar valleys
two hours flight away
such light on hills
means lock your houses,
board up your houses,
get underneath
your houses.

MUNITIONS

Since its ancient civil battles,
this place has seen no blood.

An accident of history let
the common thorns snag rabbit fur,

and nothing else. But if evil
is in absence, here is evidence:

that thorn bush, with its vascular
clutch of red wires, still ticking;

rain coming over the downs,
drumming us into our houses;

petrified skulls, hips and shields
under knuckling streams;

and in the warning bark of deer
a one-off, misplaced human cry.

SORTIES

All day, F1-11s split
the downs, rehearsing war.
Now, in their silent wake

(not an absence of noise,
but real, present quiet:
monastral green and terre-verte,

oak, ash, elder,
in an endless exhale,
and our slow milking lungs),

a seagull flags the hills
in search of herring,
fifty miles inland.

PROTECT AND SURVIVE

This is a walled city.
Its people have their own schools,
their own food flown in
to fill their own stores.

Once a month, children file
from their classes and clap
by Hangar 202 as home
is towed in from the Galaxies.

They have imported geography –
4th Avenue, 2nd Street West,
Main Street USA.
They have a theater, no theatre.

Even the hydrants
are from distant sidewalks.
Are these the first settlers,
toe-hold for a colony?

Or is it a Masada,
besieged by barbarians
on the chalk plains of Berkshire;
a pill and prayer in every pocket.

THE BATON

Melissa's nightmare is this:

her father home from work,
film-badge pinned to his lapel,
clouded by too many hours
in Aldermaston's hot labs.

He kisses Melissa, Jason, Lisa;
sets his briefcase on the table,
invites them to peer inside
between buff files.

Smooth, blue-grey, hard as iron,
is a cylinder of Cobalt 60
rolled in newspaper.
'Go on, unwrap it.'

A STORM

One sultry night a flock of Chinooks
judders in across our rooftops,
heralding a storm, pulling dark clouds
through the green sky.

All week, heat has been desperate;
you could snap it in your fingers.
Swallows wheeled higher by the day
to try to break the tension.

Now, the whole town lies
with curtains open, watching light
catch darkness unawares,
each bolt a snapshot of a secret room:

the jacket on a chair-back,
the ready-packed bag,
the witnesses –
silent ghosts with eyes all pupil.

Hidden in the thunder
was the throttle of huge planes;
Starlifters, Galaxies,
guided in by Chinooks.

Were these the first payloads,
still in their swaddling, factory-fresh?
There would be no announcement.
Everyone knew it was soon.

PAYLOAD

14th November 1983

After all the portents – storms, cortèges, sirens –
Cruise came on a brief November day as light was failing.

First on the list of victims was a Stroud Green man
– a loss-adjuster on long-term sick – whose cottage

collapsed beneath the Galaxies' thunderous final descent.
He had spent weeks sanding roof beams,

so his home stood in a skeleton as fragile as his nerves.
Was he making a seismograph, or his own mausoleum?

If asked, he would have said: '*I have to make it smooth.*'

SUMMER ADVENT

Oh come, oh come. They waited. Then summer snow began to fall, not a blizzard, but light flakes settling on the playing field. Jason Jones was in a history class. Everyone gazed at the hot azure sky which gave nothing away. One boy said it was ash from the linings of jet engines, but no one had seen it before. Some mornings a jet fuel stench would hang in the air, but never this snow. This was the day the F1-11s left the base, and this was their parting gift to 5P1, because of all the prefab overspill classrooms at the back of the school, theirs was the only one to get this dusting of jet white like a charmed circle. Mr Murphy told them not to touch it, but at break Jason tried to pick some up. It was so dry, so delicate, that as soon as he held it he lost it. Those snowflakes were too fragile for this world. He filled his pockets, but they were empty.

*

After the jets left, everything changed. Security tightened around the base. Deep within it, just visible from the perimeter fence, the Common was being recast. Long barrows appeared — burial mounds for warheads. Then the missile men came, and then the women in their makeshift tents outside the gates. They changed things too. A-Gate, B-Gate, C-Gate, became Yellow Gate, Woad Gate, Green, Violet. As soon as Jason got his driving licence, he circled the base in his father's Avenger. Bury's Bank Road was airbrushed off the maps, but locals knew it, and it took them winding and chicaning round the whole base, hugging the perimeter fence, dark between thick trees one minute, blinding with searchlights the next. Sometimes boy-racers stopped at Blue, or Green, or Yellow Gate and threw stones at the tents. Some nights on that road, especially late, they picked up a mimic on the other side of the wire, the USAF dancing with them, slowing and quickening when they did. Jason parked and stared them out. He flicked the wipers and the windscreen full of blue lights cleared, leaving one tight glass of blue like a strong drink, balanced on the roof of the disappearing police car.

★

Jason started wearing his USAF tunic to school. He was told he had to wear school uniform, so he wore his blazer over it. Apart from that, he was never in trouble. He worked hard, and talked a lot about discipline. He reported boys who brought drugs into school, and when he could, he borrowed his dad's car at night and drove up and down Bury's Bank Road by the base. He often parked near Blue Gate, where Helen – sister of a boy in his school year – had crossed the line and pitched her tent. It was as weird and as treacherous as joining the USAF. He shouted at her until he was hoarse.

III

FRIENDLY FIRE

'One of the most striking features of the airbase flora are the chalk-loving species growing alongside the former runways and thriving in conditions created by lime leaching from the concrete. The spring-fed gullies that cut into the ridge contain mire and ancient alder coppice. The southern slopes of the Commons are predominantly wooded with derelict coppice and pasture woodland.'

– Green Ways: Berkshire's Rights of Way Magazine,
Issue No. 4, Summer 1999

GROUND ZERO

Everyone agreed that here at target one
we would be woken by a drone,
a light plane at the end of its tether;
then a sputter, then a whistling fall.

After that, opinion split:
some thought we'd hear the impact,
rush to windows, be transfigured
before we were vaporised.

Others thought that too romantic.
For them, it would be drone, sputter, fall,
then one white-out instant of ultimate light,
the word *heat*; all words, obsolete.

Romantics spoke of hot flesh curling
off the bone like slow-cooked roast,
but knifeless. They warned of screams,
fires, fallout, refugees.

For purists, this undersold the light,
which would create in one split-second starburst,
worlds of glass beyond all melt or scorch.
We would be translucent statues of ourselves:

an instant ice Pompeii, one standing,
one sleeping, one in mid-step through a clear room.
Even purists liked to think there might
be relics in this crystalline metropolis:

the diamond styluses of hi-fis,
barely visible, suspended like lost pulses;
and fillings, melted and reset on glass chins
like gold and silver drool.

Each morning after, as the nuclear
winter sun peers through us all,
just imagine the fibre-optic frenzy
connecting us, unwitnessed;

then as the wind gathers pace
with the seasons, it scrubs us with its
hair shirt of sand grains, and a million
tiny scratches render us opaque again.

DUMMY RUNS

Some claimed the convoy
had passed them in the night:
the massive dark throat of its engines,
tinted glass cabs, pet-names
painted on the launchers' flanks:
Bates Motel, *Everyday Torture*,
Armageddon Express . . .

The next day we would search
the local woods for tread marks,
wild garlic shocked into scent,
coconut smells of gorse in heat,
peacock butterflies as volatile
as touchpaper.

THE TOE-RING

After school we got our first glimpse:
hair was pelt, tight-matted;
clothes russet, khaki, loose and long.
They bought two heavy tablets
of chocolate – one dark, one light.

These were the women we had heard about,
in town for supplies for their new camp,
their makeshift tents and tepees.

One was young, her feet were younger;
slim and smooth and coated in mud,
bare on the shop tiles. She wore a silver hoop
on the long toe of her left foot,
a secret sign of marriage or vocation
worn by nomads from the high plains.

They left a scent of cough-sweets.
Maybe there was no chocolate.
Perhaps her feet were tanned with it.

THE STAR

Each Christmas, a great star shone
above the base: fluorescent, bolted
to the water-tower for the festive
fortnight. It looked like a cross,

was big enough to hold a man,
but held a shape in light instead,
like an angel: a radioactive angel
glowing in the northern sky.

FEAST OF THE INNOCENTS

Turncoats you could count on a hand:
the Texan gate-guard who went native,
bought a smallholding in Cold Ash;
the local girl who took to wheeling
prams full of supplies to peace camps,
then left school and pitched her tent;
cats who took a meal and name from anyone.
Otherwise, nobody crossed the lines
between USAF, peace camps, locals.

What was needed was a latter-day
Feast of the Innocents, when children
were pilots for a day, when airmen cut
their own fence and held hands round the silos.
In the venerable footsteps of boy bishops,
Colonel Jason Jones – in finery –
would taunt the powers all morning,
launch a pre-emptive strike on the world
after lunch, drink the bar dry
then cleave his palate with a gun.

YULE BALL

The Colonel sent a Sergeant
to drive the band to play the Ball.
So here are the *Cruise Missiles*
in a USAF bus, held up at Main Gate
by a girl with a gun doing her job.

The driver stops drumming
with his fingers on the steering wheel
to glance around, see she is not coming
yet, and light a cigarette from a soft
pack of Marlboro imports.

Bence is scheming in the back:
If we can slip security
we'll stash the Christmas star
in with the amps and drums and pass
it off as a part of our stage-set.

It wants to go, that star,
he hears it buzzing with frustration,
tethered to the water-tower,
held back from its solemn duty
always to point to the truth.

THE RAM-RAID

On their 21st, the Moss twins
– already orphans – tried to burst
the fence in a hot-wired car:
a kamikaze dash to the silos.

But they never reached
the razor wire, armed guards,
atom-proof concrete.
The perimeter fence alone
turned and torched the car.
When the twins did not come back,
their empty house went live.

Burst pipes, broken tanks,
water-papered walls
and loose wires conjured lightning,
arcing and cracking across rooms.
At night, the house flickered,
wet and live with eel electrons.
Nobody dared go in.

In the end, their uncle
– still in black and mourning –
waded in with the deceptive
insouciance of those who work
with voltage; cigarette on lip,
one hand in a pocket so as not
to make a circuit of himself.

He found the master switch
and put the house to sleep,
then sat down as the charge
died all around him.

TENTED VILLAGE

Cooking fires are done,
charcoal crumbles into mud.

Last night's flames died alone,
unaided by the firemen of the M.O.D.

The benders are quiet, save the flag
flap of loose-tethered canvas.

Armies of women sleep at each gate,
in the tear-ducts of the base,

rucksacks packed for the weekly
6 a.m. eviction. Radio, tin mug, diary;

refugee relics tied to wrists in bags
to keep them from the bailiffs.

This is the night before battle.
They are King Richard's or Henry's forces,

praying and cursing in their dreams,
as spies bring news from the enemy camp.

Yet all nights are the night before.
The battle never comes.

A GHOST-TREE

When the Common bore no trees –
all runway, hangar, mound,
Jason glimpsed one night a ghost-tree

– a leafless, towering ash –
a shade caught in his headlamps on
the wrong side of the wire.

Yet the moment he slowed to take it in,
to park and listen to its whispered polemics,
it collapsed into its shadow.

Ash into ashes.
If he could reach through the fence,
he would have licked a finger,

dabbed it in the shadow, and daubed
his forehead as an amulet against
the worlds of fire the base contained.

THE SACRIFICE

Sirens in the small hours:
in come the Cadillacs and Chryslers,
the families who live outside.

Yellow, to red, to black alert;
troops in masks and radiation suits
usher cars through Main Gate.

Yellow Gate women stagger
from their tents and squat in the road
to scupper this night exercise,

but only the Colonel knows for sure
if this is a rehearsal, or the big bang.
Either way, it must feel real.

The men who drive are silent
as they run through their procedures,
steer round women in the road.

Those huddled women are silent
because of the kids in the back of the cars;
moth-frail in night clothes, white with fear.

One girl in particular, sobs
in her mother's arms, old enough to know
what this could mean, young enough

to wonder what her role could be,
the Colonel's daughter, deeply loved,
who somehow has to save the world.

DEPOSITION

This was easy. A ready ladder
bolted to the water-tower, no police
in sight, no nails in the star.

They yanked the plug out of its back,
loosened its wire stirrups,
eased it down to earth.

Sirens raced towards some smoke
at Blue Gate. No one saw the Star
of Bethlehem stolen from the sky.

In a garage, under blankets, days later
still it glowed. They threw it
into the canal, but it floated.

They were scared to bury it
in case its iridescence seeped
into the soil.

In the end, they drove up to the base
and threw it back like an inedible fish.
It broke into a plague of fireflies in the grass.

FRIENDLY FIRE

Words first, but they never hurt;
shouting from the cars at night:
'Fucking dykes! Go fuck yourselves!'

Then it was sticks and stones,
cars parked and the boys out,
chucking at the tents.

Then rotten fruit, gloved and held
by saggy drumskin roofs,
like lurid, stinking manna.

Then one night it was petrol,
a milk bottle, a lit rag.
'This'll warm you. Bitches.'

No one was ever caught.
'Three of them. Smart clothes.
Green Avenger. Local accents.'

MELISSA JONES

Once, they found a schoolgirl
in a pillbox hermitage by Guyer's Lock.
Curled inside the concrete snail-shell
— built to quash invasion by canal —
she had brought her own relics:

chocolate, candles, blankets,
a clutch of her mother's Valium
knotted in a yellow duster,
a torn-out book of Genesis.

She had told friends that she never slept,
kept a night-long vigil for a sound
like an aeroplane but very fast and falling.
All here would be melt and white
in the first moment of the third war.
So she ran and hid, never came back.

Rumour had it she was living
like Eve in a copse by the Kennet,
dressed in rags, eating birds and blackberries;
a feral girl with juice-dark hands,
living from pillbox to pillbox.

THE LIST

Victims of the Blue Gate fire
which tore through plastic, canvas, wool:

Sal, who lost the last and truest
photo of her mother;

Georgia, who was haunted
by the smell of petrol ever after;

Helen, who went back to snatch
her diary and became the monster

in the mirror she had always feared,
her face recast into a mask;

Melissa, who knew that her brother
threw the bottle-bomb, but did not tell;

Pastor Jude, the USAF chaplain,
who took it as a sign of the end-times

but was not ready; and the subtle
calculus of light versus darkness,

which hangs in a balance as delicate as cloud,
and slips another shade towards despair.

STRANGE MEETING

'I am the enemy you killed, my friend.'
                              Wilfred Owen

In accordance with the armistice,
a Russian MIG could drop
– at barely two hours' notice –
on the peaceful plains of Berkshire,

so Soviet inspectors could
confirm the silos' emptiness,
could stamp, clap, shout,
to check the echo's fullness,

could comb the place for hide or hair
of Cruise, tell-tale signs of sudden
recent moves, the warm prints
of missiles in their midden.

Of course, the real deal was
a quick stroll through the silos,
then the finest wines, a junket,
bilingual toasts to absent friends.

Next morning, back to Russia
with sore heads and a plane full
of deadly contraband: *Pepsi,
Hustler, Levis, Springsteen, Bud.*

IV

HYPOCENTRE

'When all has finally been made safe, the perimeter fence will be removed. Stock fencing will be erected to enable the Common to be managed through grazing and there will be numerous public access points. Providing a habitat for many rare and endangered species, the Common will prove a haven for local wildlife as well as a place of enjoyment for local people.'

– Greenham Common Trust Newsletter,
Winter 1999

LAMENT

How far she has fallen, naked and bled,
this once majestic city, fist-tight fortress.

Her tears swamp her chalk bed,
her gully streams are overwhelmed.

Her enemies have strewn salt
in the streets where nothing breathes.

Her pregnant silos have been slit,
gestating young dismembered,

before their maiden flights.
Her once proud gates gape open,

she is overrun with fruitfulness:
raspberries, blackberries, elder caviar,

painted ladies, commas, peacocks,
sundews, orchids, bittercress.

In her shattered wine-halls,
vestigial barracks, shelled offices,

where feral dog-packs pick and piss
on bottles, plaster, coats, shoes,

wood and skylarks stake out
a new empire of the air.

Soon, only a handful will recall
the warriors she raised

to face Hitler, the Kaiser, Napoleon.
Soon, the few old men with memories

will root among the scrub for kindling
and keepsakes, but in vain.

THE DISAPPEARED

for John Wells

When *détente* stormed the gates,
it found a maquette of a nation,
from hydrants to street signs;
a lost tribe of the States,
but there were precious few real relics.

This was no Masada myth,
no suicide cult of portents and fire.
They left their megaliths, their empty homes,
but not a hint of why they left,
and not a single truck or coupé.

Were they buried in their cars,
like tribal chieftains in their ships?
Were their hands lashed to the wheel
to keep the fleet on target
for the centre of the earth?

Or were they flown home
in their driving seats by Galaxies
and Starlifters, revving as the planes
touched down, back home woundless
from the cold war with a foot on the gas.

Either way, no one saw a single car
slip out on those last nights
between the Bury's Bank Road brambles
or Stroud Green's skyscraping poplars.
Nobody left by land.

NEW GREENHAM PARK

They move like ghosts across the wasteland
of numbered, nameless fortresses, dead signs:
'DANGER – Razor Wire', *'DANGER – Barbed Wire'*,
'ABSOLUTELY no access' . . . To what?
Building 260, former Officers' Canteen,
next on the demolition list. These wreckers
are locals, struggling to smash their own landscape.

The base was built for the end of the world,
so it resists hydraulic claws and hammers.
Some men feel a strange nostalgia for the sirens,
the sleepless chill as jets flew in and out,
terrors and tales of radiation sickness.

One of the wreckers – Leo – starts to wash his boots
a little longer at the end of each day.
He breaks protocol and talks to a warden
who tells him of small victories:
five types of berry bejewelling Shed 276,
homecoming black-caps and nightingales.

She tells him through a face recast by fire.
There are rumours – Falklands veteran,
firework accident, but she never talks of burns,
only of her dream of common land come home.
Leo wishes he could say this:

'If you brought Komodo Dragons, Lovebirds
and Banana Groves to this heath, no locals would come
here more than once, and even then to lay a ghost.
They will wear strings of garlic under jackets,
will finger childhood relics – toy cars, dolls' hands,
shells – as touchstones in their pockets.'

WOAD

This is the final shame
for Greenham's derelict city:

its hollow school, its shells of stores,
its bar without strangers or regulars.

This is a wild-west fantasy
for stag weekenders, management trainees,

stalking the ghost-town with paintballs.
They turn the schoolroom blackboards blue.

They wear bruises which begin
on clothes and sink through to the skin.

Each bruise is a life lost in this bloodless
massacre, past lives tattooed into them

like light from dead stars.
Outside, old walls are relief maps;

once they charted brick-red deserts,
then came blue oases, then whole lakes.

Now each wall is an ocean map, a prophecy
of ice-caps melted, nations overwhelmed.

Between these royal-blue buildings,
dodging paintballs, pheasants

from the woods drift in and flap for cover.
Game birds shot at Greenham are not killed

but winged, scuttled into new lives
as cobalt birds of paradise.

RESTORATION

Now Europe's longest runway is uprooted.
It resists, like the rest of the base,
but hydraulic fists smash it
into concrete boulders in a mud canal.

Rumour is this rubble will become
hardcore for the bypass
as it tears a stripe through ancient woodlands
leaving Newbury unscathed.

That pulverised runway
will make car headlamps obsolete.
It's the future, a road that generates
its own subtle light as it ushers us all

through Penn Wood and the Chase
towards the celestial city.

FAUNA

It is the first day of the first
spring since the missiles left.
In the tight, hardy clumps of scrub
around the silos, big yellow
butterflies are ribbons on the green.

Resurrection yes,
but they are *sulphur* yellow,
and their name is Brimstone.
They could have burst from the silos
when the doors were opened.

SECOND STRIKE

This was the real Trojan horse,
no bolt-cutters in the chain-link fence,
but a hot-wired Fiat Uno,
joy-ridden in through Yellow Gate,
dumped on the shattered runway
outside the Command Centre.

'LOCALS INVADE BASE' . . .
but too late. Troy was empty.
The walled city was a wasteland.
Pointless graffiti sprayed on the car:
'Fuck you yanks, and kiss my arse.'
'Catch us if you can.' No one tried,
so they rode the runway scree
until the tyres were seaweed straps,
then threw a hunk of concrete
through the windscreen,
which settled in the driver's seat,
adorned with blue glass lozenges.

They stripped it of its number plates
and walked home through Green Gate
as the engine ticked behind them.

WARLORDS IN WAITING

The silos themselves, the very hearts,
deep within the base, would take generations
to destroy, so they have been abandoned.

Six long barrows, in two rows,
grass-covered, rounded down at one end,
concrete-stepped and gated at the other,
sacred chambers, works of giants.

Picture spring after a nuclear winter:
explorers hacking through the bramble
and brush discover sealed tombs
of the six great kings of ancient Britain.

COMMON TOAD

Not so common here for decades
while the grass was crew-cut twice a week,

but now this heathland flourishes,
and banished creatures crawl back

through the fence-holes. There are setbacks.
Every morning Helen takes a walk

by the silos where rabbits have tunnelled
beneath rusting razor wire

and made homes in the concrete caves.
Where the broken runway meets the wire

she found a headless toad, splayed
and shrivelled, victim of the scrawny cats

which lead a life half on the common,
and half in warm homes on the estate.

The toad's bitter skin saved its body,
spat out like a dried-up chamois,

parched as a scar, the same tight foreign
tissue which now coats Helen's face.

That is why she cannot scrape away
this faceless corpse, but monitors its changes,

especially on wet days, when the rain
revivifies the toad until it puffs up

and occupies its form again,
at home in the true fit of its skin.

ENDGAME

Pastor Jude (baptised Judas,
his father's revenge on the Church)
leaves his escorts at the cabin
where business park turns moonscape.
He tiptoes down the runway's
stepping stones, between the stinking
heaps of gravel laced with jet fuel,
and he wonders why we are still here.

Twenty years ago, when he was USAF
chaplain, his sermons were about
the last days of the world, the tribulation.
'Be wakeful, be ready, believe.
Time will end before we've said it's soon.'
By now, the faithful should be raptured
into heaven, but nobody is missing.
He knows. He counts the faithful.

By now the final battle should be on,
but here, without a breach of peace,
his old base has turned wasteland:
padlocks and hasps on every rusted door,
his tin-shed chapel flattened,
and Hangar 202 in which he tried,
one Easter Sunday, to pluck last-minute
doubters from hell's flames – all gone.

Is this hell? Barren and cold,
left empty by a God of mercy.
Or (a heresy even to think it)
has the world been jilted at the altar,
robbed of its rightful apocalypse.
Jude picks three ripe blackberries
from a bush where his home once stood,
then leaves like a man leaves a desert.

GRAVE GOODS

When the Cruises were gone,
their tombs were cleaned out
– dank and dark – no ice metal
shells to turn the earth's breath
into condensation.

Under the missiles they found
skeletons, chattels and gold torques,
pools alive with blind white fish.
Deeper still, chalk animals
that never reached the surface.

DEUS EX MACHINA – I

As the cold war is converted
to a multimedia museum,
pika – looking old on photographs –
is now at work on origins, not ends.

In a Long Island laboratory,
tests begin on a nuclear accelerator,
a Relativistic Heavy Ion Collider
a Big Bang Machine.

One October day – when leaves
reveal their paper imagos –
Long Island starts to replicate
the moment of creation.

Atoms of gold are skinned
and smashed into each other
at light-speed. Each collision
generates a fireball of plasma,

hotter than the hearts of stars
– a trillion degrees – hotter than
anything has been since
the universe was born.

As the plasma cools, it breathes
a shower of particles
and suddenly – a risk the physicists
assessed and found too small to heed –

strange quarks are formed,
the unstable agents of creation
and apocalypse. There is no time
for rescue or repentance.

Pika is glimpsed on Long Island,
then grows in an instant
to overwhelm us all: the world
consumed by its beginning.

THE FENCE

The first vast computers ran
on memories made of chain-mail,
metal fabric woven in the old mills.
Small wonder then, that these
five miles of chain-link fence
are one unravelled sheet of memory:

tokens, ribbons, prayers
tied into it for twenty years;
spectral paint-can symbols,
rushed episiotomies performed
by peace-camp midwives,
and the barbed-wire top
traced with threads and DNA.

Now, in its senility,
the base has lost whole chapters,
bailed up like a harvest
between pointless concrete posts
like standing stones.
There is no longer any difference
between outside and in.

REMNANT

On the A339 to Basingstoke:
one caravan with hanging baskets,

three feral cats and a tame thrush.
one makeshift memory garden,

one *No More Hiroshimas* banner,
one maroon estate car rusted shut.

No more evictions. Two women,
becalmed by the absence of the end.

DEUS EX MACHINA – II

Pika falls captive to the internet,
harnessed by the new illuminati
to communicate light-speed.

On a sharp October day – when
summer's eggshell glaze begins to crack –
the worldwide teleconference

hits zenith, and past and future
die in a moment of ultimate
simultaneous inertia:

everyone watching everyone else
in a live relay at *pika*-speed,
and the journey suddenly over.

A GIFT HORSE

Rogation Sunday: ten locals beat
the bounds of the fenceless common.

One Greenham farmer staked his ancient
claim to graze beasts on this wasteland:

'Each commoner can turn out
47 cattle, 17 goats, 16 ponies, 12 horses,

6 sheep, 4 pigs, 2 ducks, 2 geese
and donkeys without limit.'

The farmer made his point with sheep
and with a troupe of circus horses out to grass.

Now each shout or slammed
door sets the lead cob off in old routines

– a dozen team-mates circling, crossing –
pointlessly rehearsing.

Stunned by dusk after a stabled life,
they usher in nightfall rock-still.

From the road, these statues
mesmerise, as drivers strain to tell

live horses from abandoned gifts,
chock-full of soldiers waiting for the dark.

THE WANDERER

On a still October day – when
bonfires spin the summer into cloud –
Jason Jones, back after a decade,
takes time out at Blue Gate
on his way to Pyle Hill woods.

Blue camp-site is black with mud
and cinders, even after all these years.
Giant concrete boulders – to ensure
no tents return – are odd now
as freak hailstones.

In the woods, Jason heaps up sticks,
tips a can of lighter fuel,
drops a match, shrugs off his olive
air-force jacket, hangs it on the flames
as on a chair-back.

BLACKOUT

Over the brow of a track,
through three fields and two gates,
we saw the fullest moon,
its own grey continents
mapped out across its face.

They say the moon has no light
of its own, but now I know
the moon contains the sun,
as pregnant as the fat ewes
watchful, aching under trees.

It's like a chinese lantern,
and its hide's so thick
that it holds that scalding child
for one night at a time inside
before new light burns out.